A Tribute to
THE YOUNG AT HEART

PEGGY PARISH

By Jill C. Wheeler

Published by Abdo & Daughters, 4940 Viking Drive, Suite 622, Edina, Minnesota 55435.

Copyright © 1997 by Abdo Consulting Group, Inc., Pentagon Tower, P.O. Box 36036, Minneapolis, Minnesota 55435 USA. International copyrights reserved in all countries. No part of this book may be reproduced in any form without written permission from the publisher.

Printed in the United States.

Cover and Interior Photo credits: Harper Collins Publishers
Herman Parish

Special Thanks to Herman Parish and family for providing photos of Peggy Parish.

Edited by Julie Berg

Library of Congress Cataloging-in-Publication Data

Wheeler, Jill C., 1964-
    Peggy Parish / Jill C. Wheeler.
    p.   cm. -- (A tribute to the young at heart)
    Includes Index
    Summary: A biography of the author of the well-loved "Amelia Bedelia" books.

    ISBN 1-56239-785-0

    1. Parish, Peggy--Biography--Juvenile literature. 2. Women authors, American --20th century--Biography--Juvenile literature. 3. Children's stories--Author-ship--Juvenile literature. [1. Parish, Peggy. 2. Authors, American. 3. Women --Biography.] I. Title. II. Series.
PS3566.A756Z9   1997
813' .54--dc21
[B]   96-29789
                                            CIP
                                            AC

Table of Contents

LITERALLY SPEAKING

English can be a very funny language. What if you did everything people told you to do—exactly as they told you?

Say they told you to make a sponge cake. Would you put sponge pieces in the cake batter? What if they told you to dress the turkey? Would you put clothes on it? How about if they told you to draw the drapes? Would you get out your sketchpad?

Those are just some of the questions that went through Peggy Parish's mind. Parish loved the English language. She also could laugh at it. She liked to find fun new ways to teach children about language. One way was through writing books for them.

Parish is the creator of Amelia Bedelia. Amelia Bedelia is

America's favorite scatter-brained maid. When her employers tell her to do something, she takes it literally. That means to understand words as people normally use them. Yet often we must look at what people mean when they say certain words. Sometimes what they say and what they mean are different.

Parish had lots of fun twisting words with Amelia Bedelia. Most people know her for those books. Yet during her career, she wrote more than 60 books. Some were books about how to do crafts. Some were mysteries. Some were books about events in history. No matter what the topic, children enjoyed reading Parish's books. People have bought more than seven million copies of her books.

"Children have always been my life," Parish says. "So writing stories for children came naturally. I do have special feelings about writing for children. I don't try to teach anything in my stories—I write for fun."

TELL ME A STORY

Parish was born Margaret Cecile Parish on July 14, 1927, in Manning, South Carolina. In those days, Manning was just a small town. "Everybody knew everybody," Parish recalls of her hometown. "Life centered around the churches and schools." It was a pleasant, quiet life for Peggy, her brother Stanley, and her parents, Herman and Cecile.

Peggy Parish was often sick as a child. Fortunately, many people read stories to her. They wanted to help her feel better. She loved hearing the stories. She would ask for more and more.

Besides reading, Parish enjoyed going to school. She decided she wanted to be a teacher. She enrolled at the University of South Carolina. She graduated in 1948 with a degree in English. Then she moved to Texhoma, Texas, near the Oklahoma border. Parish taught English and creative dancing in the part of Oklahoma known as the panhandle. The panhandle sticks out, into Texas.

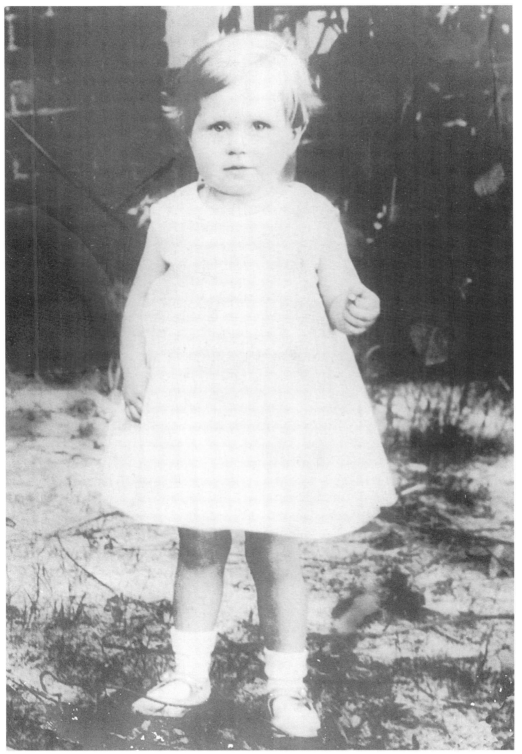

Peggy Parish at two years old.

Eventually, she moved to Kentucky. There she taught third graders whose parents worked in the local coal mines.

Finally, she moved to New York City. Her first job there was with the Girl Scouts of America. Then she got a job teaching third grade at the private Dalton School in Manhattan. She taught at Dalton for more than 15 years.

Parish began writing while teaching at Dalton. She never had taken formal classes in writing before. Writing simply had come easily to her. At first, her manuscripts came back rejected after she sent them off to publishers. Then friends introduced her to some editors. The editors helped her with her first books.

Her first big break came in 1962. That was the year she published *My Golden Book of Manners*. The famous illustrator Richard Scarry drew the pictures for Parish's book. The next year was 1963. That year, Parish introduced a very special person to the world of literature. Her name was Amelia Bedelia.

HELLO AMELIA BEDELIA!

Parish enjoyed spending time with her students at Dalton School. Sometimes they amazed her with how smart they were. For example, she would say "Let's call the roll." They might respond with a giggle and call, "Hey, Roll!" Then they would ask her if she really meant to say that.

Her students' remarks got Parish thinking. What if there was a character who took everything people said literally? That's how Amelia Bedelia was born.

Amelia is a maid who works for Mr. and Mrs. Rogers. Her problem is that she takes what they say very literally. Sometimes that gets her into trouble. In *Amelia Bedelia*, the Rogers ask her to dust the furniture. She does—by sprinkling dust on the furniture instead of wiping it off. They also ask her to change the towels. She does—by cutting them into different shapes.

After Parish wrote *Amelia Bedelia*, she was nervous about sending it to a publisher. She wasn't sure anyone would like it. She was wrong. The book was a big hit. In fact, all the Amelia Bedelia books are popular books in the easy-to-read section.

Parish never forgot about her students "calling the roll," either. She had Amelia Bedelia do that in *Teach Us, Amelia Bedelia*.

Parish sometimes had to do unusual research for her books. In one Amelia Bedelia book, she had Amelia making a sponge cake. Of course, Amelia wanted to use real sponges. Parish had to give it a try to see how it would work!

"The things I have Amelia Bedelia do must be plausible," Parish says. "When I was writing *Good Work, Amelia Bedelia*, I thought of having her make a sponge cake in her own inimitable way. So, I spent one afternoon in the kitchen snipping pieces of a sponge into a cake batter. I didn't know whether it would get gooey, burn up, or do what I hoped—stay like a sponge. Fortunately, the sponge stayed like a sponge and that's the way it is in the book."

In 1964, Parish published *Thank You, Amelia Bedelia.* Two years later, she wrote *Amelia Bedelia and the Surprise Shower.* Parish would go on to write 10 more Amelia Bedelia books.

Peggy Parish in the 1940s.

LAUGHING AND LEARNING

Parish said she thought there were several reasons why kids love Amelia Bedelia. "Perhaps in Amelia Bedelia children have the opportunity to laugh at adults," she said. She's quick to admit that adults often do things that don't make sense. Also, Amelia often makes mistakes. That teaches kids that it's OK to make mistakes.

The Amelia Bedelia books teach kids about words, too. They learn about homonyms. Homonyms are words that mean different things, but sound the same, such as steak and stake. In *Amelia Bedelia Helps Out*, Amelia's employer tells her to stake the beans. Her employer wants her to tie the bean plants to stakes in the ground. However, Amelia ties a piece of beef steak to each plant instead.

Amelia Bedelia also teaches readers about homographs. Homographs are words that are spelled the same but mean different things depending on how you use them. One such word is dust. People dust furniture by taking the dust off of it. When you dust plants for bugs, you put a special dust on the plants that the bugs don't like. In *Amelia Bedelia Helps Out*, Amelia dusts bugs the way people dust furniture. She takes them off the plants and brushes them with a feather duster!

Teachers all over the nation have used the Amelia Bedelia books to help their students learn just how funny the English language can be. Parish said she liked knowing her books were helping out in classrooms like the ones in which she taught.

INDIANS, MYSTERIES, AND MORE

While most people know Parish best for Amelia Bedelia, she wrote many other books as well.

After *My Golden Book of Manners*, Parish wrote *Good Hunting, Little Indian* and *Let's Be Indians*. *Good Hunting, Little Indian* is the story of a young Native American boy and his quest to be a hunter. Like the Amelia Bedelia tales, the story contains its share of twists and turns. *Let's Be Indians* shows readers how to make Native American costumes, toys, and games.

Parish enjoyed writing about Native Americans. She had heard many stories about them as a child. Their lifestyle fascinated her. However, many people later criticized her writings about Native Americans. They said they were not true to the Native American culture. Editors have updated some of Parish's books to be more accurate to the Native American culture.

Amelia Bedelia is not the only series of books that Parish has written. She also wrote a series about a tough, little old lady named Granny Guntry. Granny finds herself in many hair-raising situations—and her readers love it. She also has many dealings with Native Americans.

Parish also wrote many stand-alone books. Often, the characters' own confusion gets them in trouble. In *Mr. Adams's Mistake*, Mr. Adams is too proud to get glasses. Yet his job is to find children who should be in school but aren't. Mr. Adams finds a monkey he thinks is a child. He takes the monkey to school. The monkey gets into all kinds of trouble.

In *Be Ready at Eight*, absent-minded Miss Molly can't remember why there's a string around her finger. She knows she's supposed to remember that it's a special day. Yet why is it special? She spends the whole day trying to figure out her own mystery.

Mysteries are a central part of another of Parish's series. She created and wrote a series of mysteries about the three Roberts children—Liza, Bill, and Jed. In their first book, *Key to the Treasure*, the three set out on a treasure hunt. In *Clues in the Woods*, several items mysteriously disappear from their home. The book tells of their quest to solve the mystery. In *Haunted House*, Liza, Bill, and Jed's family move into a house they think is haunted. They find a series of clues they must decode to get to the heart of the secret.

Peggy Parish in the mid 1960s.

DINOSAURS AND CRAFTS

Parish also wrote many nonfiction books. She shared her love of crafts with her readers in *Costumes to Make* and *Sheet Magic: Games, Toys, and Gifts from Old Sheets*. In *Costumes to Make*, Parish offers step-by-step instructions for making outfits for parties, plays, or even Halloween. *Sheet Magic* shows how to use old sheets for everything from creative games to pretend parachutes. Parish also wrote a craft book on mobiles, and several craft books specifically for the holiday season.

Parish liked writing to help children understand more about the world around them. Her book *Dinosaur Time* told all about dinosaurs. The book was published in 1974. *School Library Journal* named it one of the best books of the year. *Dinosaur Time* also received the Garden State Children's Book Award from the state of New Jersey. She wrote another nonfiction book about grain in 1965. She titled it *The Story of Grains: Wheat, Corn, and Rice*.

After all of that, does Parish have a favorite book? No, she said. "Each one is my child."

Peggy Parish in 1970 during a newspaper interview.

THE BUSINESS OF WRITING

In her spare time, Parish enjoyed working in her garden. She often got ideas for more stories while she was weeding. Then, when it got too hot to work outside, she went inside and wrote down the ideas she had. Some of them turned into stories.

Her many cats also provided her with inspiration for stories. She called one of them *The Cats' Burglar*. The book is about nine cats that foil a burglar.

Parish wrote other books about pets, too. One is called *Scruffy*. In the book, a young boy goes to an animal shelter to choose a pet cat. At the shelter, he learns about the responsibilities of caring for a pet. In *No More Monsters For Me*, a girl adopts a monster because her mother won't let her have a pet. But when the monster gets too big, her mother agrees to let her have a cat instead.

Parish says writing books isn't always easy. "I must get the story worked out in my mind before I can bring it to paper," she said. "I often lie in bed for hours at a time, staring at the ceiling, working very hard on a book."

"Sometimes it seems to take forever to plan and write a book," Parish says. "Other times the plot for a book seems to pop out of no place begging to be put down on paper. This is what happened with *Too Many Rabbits*. It required no conscious effort on my part. The words just seemed to flow and I really enjoyed writing it."

"I wish this could happen more often, but it has happened only a couple of times for me. Usually a book takes a lot of thinking, planning, and just hard work in writing and rewriting time and time again before it's ready to be published."

Even though she believes in education, Parish thinks it's very important that books be fun to read. "I won't read a book I don't like," she said. "So why should children be forced to do so?" She encouraged all of her young readers to read as much as they could. "All the skills needed to read can be taught outside of textbooks," she said. "If schools taught children to read through the books they are interested in, then we would not have non-readers. Children will only become lifelong readers by discovering the joy in books."

Peggy Parish likes gardening.

HOME AGAIN

In 1972, after many years in New York City, Parish returned to South Carolina. She continued writing books there. She spoke to library associations and children's education groups. She even ran a children's book review service.

Some people saw her on television. She reviewed children's books for the "Carolina Today" TV show in Columbia, South Carolina.

Once in a while, she would run into her old teachers. Parish's first grade teacher was very special to her. Parish dedicated the book *Teach Us, Amelia Bedelia* to her. The dedication reads, "For Miss Rose, my first grade teacher, who introduced me to the magic of words, with love."

Great aunt Peggy Parish with her grand
nephew Philip Rogers Parish.

HAPPY BIRTHDAY, AMELIA BEDELIA

1988 was a special year for Parish. It was Amelia Bedelia's 25th birthday! Parish's publishers decided to celebrate this special occasion.

To celebrate, the publishers sent special mailboxes to hundreds of bookstores and libraries. Then the publishers, bookstores, and libraries asked children to put birthday wishes for Amelia Bedelia in the mailboxes. The cards and letters poured in.

Parish's publishers began receiving the contents of those mailboxes in August 1988. Over the next few months, thousands of letters and drawings from children poured in. The children told how they had read and loved books about Amelia Bedelia. Even at age 25, Amelia Bedelia was still a favorite among young readers.

The last official portrait of Peggy Parish, taken at her church in Manning, South Carolina.

A NEW CHAPTER BEGINS

Shortly after Amelia's birthday celebration, Parish was rushed to a hospital in her hometown of Manning, South Carolina. She died there of a ruptured abdominal aneurysm. An aneurysm is a weak place inside the body that can burst unexpectedly. Parish died on November 19, 1988.

Just months before, her 12th Amelia Bedelia book had come out. She called it *Amelia Bedelia's Family Album*. In her 61 years, she had written more than 30 books for children.

Fortunately for Amelia Bedelia fans, the story doesn't end there. Parish's nephew, Herman Parish, began writing more stories about Amelia Bedelia. In 1995, he published a new book. He called it *Good Driving, Amelia Bedelia*.

In the book, Mr. Rogers takes Amelia out for a driving lesson. Not surprisingly, Amelia runs into problems finding crossroads. She insists all the roads she finds are very nice! She also has trouble looking for a fork in the road. "I don't see any forks or spoons," she says.

Even if there are no more new Amelia Bedelia books, you can be sure no one will forget her. America's favorite silly maid has helped many children learn to read. She's also helped them make sense out of a very funny language.

WRITINGS

Peggy Parish is best known for her Amelia Bedelia books. Yet she wrote many books for children. Following is a list of some of her writings.

My Golden Book of Manners, Golden Press, 1962

Good Hunting, Little Indian, Young Scott Books, 1962

Amelia Bedelia, Harper, 1963

Thank You, Amelia Bedelia, Harper, 1964

The Story of Grains: Wheat, Corn, and Rice, Grosset, 1965

Let's Be Early Settlers with Daniel Boone, Harper, 1967

Little Indian, Simon & Schuster, 1968

Granny and the Indians, Macmillan, 1969

Costumes to Make, Macmillan, 1970

Snapping Turtle's All Wrong Day, Simon & Schuster, 1970

Sheet Magic: Games, Toys, and Gifts from Old Sheets, Macmillan, 1971

Play Ball, Amelia Bedelia, Harper, 1972

Too Many Rabbits, Macmillan, 1974

Dinosaur Time, Harper, 1974

Let's Celebrate: Holiday Decorations You Can Make,
  Morrow, 1976

Teach Us, Amelia Bedelia, Morrow, 1977

Mind Your Manners!, Greenwillow, 1978

Be Ready at Eight, Macmillan, 1979

No More Monsters for Me!, Harper, 1981

Mr. Adams's Mistake, Macmillan, 1982

The Cats' Burglar, Greenwillow, 1983

Amelia Bedelia Goes Camping, Greenwillow, 1985

Scruffy, Harper, 1988

GLOSSARY OF TERMS

Aneurysm — A soft spot in an artery that tends to break open.

Homograph — Two words that are spelled the same but have different meanings.

Homonyms — Two words that sound the same but are spelled differently and have different meanings.

Literally — To understand a word as people usually use it without paying attention to how it's used.

Inimitable — Not capable of being imitated.

Plausible — Something that can be believed.

INDEX